God's
Human Email

C000101190

JON GLEDHILL
Author

ISABEL WATSON
Illustrator

malcolm down
PUBLISHING

Scripture quotations taken from The Holy Bible, New International Version
(Anglicised edition) Copyright ©1979, 1984, 2011 by Biblica.
Used by permission of Hodder & Stoughton Publishers,
an Hachette UK company.
All rights reserved.

ISBN 978-1-915046-36-9

Illustrations by Isabel Watson

Printed in the UK

Endorsements

Throughout church history, illustrating and applying the bible to the present day has been a vital part of relevant gospel presentation. In this beautifully illustrated devotional book, Jon Gledhill and Isabel Watson provide rich portraits from our modern daily life with deep spiritual truths, illustrating and applying God's word in a way that will leave readers helped and hope-filled.

Regan King, Pastor of The Angel Church, Islington, London

It's such a joy to see God leading both Jon and Isabel to finish this first book. The blogs and paintings carry simple biblical truth envisaged in current settings so that even children can understand them. Simply turn to any page, look at the picture, read and narrate, it will enable you to praise God and relate with others.

Roland Lim, Director, Waterplus PTE Ltd. Singapore

This beautifully presented and illustrated book is filled with thoughtful, sometimes challenging comments based on numerous Bible stories. Keep one on your coffee table!

John Rose, Senior Administrator, Urban Saints.

This is a beautiful, creative, inspiring book bound to captivate the reader in the heart and soul. Don't just put it on your coffee table. Walk through it slowly and thoughtfully, and see how God might speak to you.

Matt Summerfield, Lead Pastor, Zeo Church, Hitchin. UK Matt Summerfield, Lead Pastor, Zeo Church, Hitchin. UK

Contents

Introduction

An emerging vision

"You will write a book."

So said a Christian leader when I was working in the middle east. I didn't think that much about this comment until I was asked by my church in England to write a blog. The blog was well received and subsequent blogs flowed.

I was then in another meeting whereby a group of prophets, who I had never met before, spoke over me, "I see you writing . . . It's like a blog or a book," "You have a gift of being able to articulate truth in ways that are easy to grasp."

It was at that point that I began to envision something like a 'book full of blogs.'

However, I felt that writing alone was not enough, and a visual impact was needed. When Jesus taught, he used visual images to help people understand truth. We say a "picture paints a thousand words." The aim of this book is to allow the reader to capture each blog written down after seeing a painting that corresponds to the writing for a few moments first. They can then ponder how to put into practice whatever they hear.

Some of the blogs are prophetic insights that I trust will inspire the reader. Others unpack parts of the bible that do not seem to be preached, or tend to be missed. The first blog on Esther was based on this.

I am so grateful for the provision of two excellent people to make the book possible: Izzy Watson has been an inspiration with her artwork and strength to overcome, as outlined in her testimony. She has been faithful in delivering the project at remarkable speed including practical assistance with editing.

Johnny Gentle has been a remarkable support. Leading in pastoral care within Kings Arms church Bedford, he decided to call me every week for one hour from the start of the COVID pandemic (2020) which is remarkable. During these times of ministry he followed the discernment of the Holy Spirit as we sought God.

The amazing thing is that at the time of writing this book during the pandemic, I had never met either Izzy or Johnny in person! God has been so good! This helps me see that God is behind it!

As you read the book you may find that some blogs are within territory you know about well. Others not so well.

I do hope and pray that you are inspired!

Jon Gledhill

A Childhood Dream – the illustrator's story

The idea of being an illustrator really appealed to me as a creative young girl, however, the 'adult world' soon dissolved that dream.

I entered university to do a teaching degree after battling two bouts of cancer throughout my school life (one aged 9, and a reoccurrence of the same brain tumour aged 17 of which also caused a stroke).

The first year went well but typically I failed a placement in the second, and the school could only do a retake in the following year during the last term. I had two terms free from study!

I consequently decided to travel on my own to Australia (which was incredible) but en route back, I had dizzy spells. At first we thought it was vertigo from the flights, however these spells increased to longer and more intense episodes and eventually mum rushed me to A&E when I couldn't even stand up. After a CT scan, I was diagnosed with brain tumour number three. Unfortunately this meant university was also stopped.

I had the new proton treatment in Florida (again an incredible experience with God holding my hand throughout), and was able to finish my degree by going into the third year of a brand new course.

After all that hassle with studying, I felt that I didn't want to teach anymore and the new course hadn't even qualified me to do this anyway. The future looked pretty hopeless.

Interestingly I was still painting throughout all of this, and was even able to paint during my stroke aged seventeen. About six years ago, and throughout my third bout of cancer, I decided I wanted to use this talent for God. I started to try and hear from him, and painted what I felt He was saying to me about my life. In addition to this, I tried to bless others with prints of these different paintings as I feel art speaks to different people in different ways.

I blessed a family with one of my paintings whilst they were going through some rough times. One of these family members (Johnny Gentle) just happened to be mentoring Jon Gledhill, who said he needed an illustrator for a book! Johnny was sat opposite the painting I'd given them at the time, and thus recommended me!

I trusted God with my life which seemed so hopeless, I am still battling dizziness and other long-term symptoms, but now I have a future as an illustrator!

I think the blog that resonated with me the most is 'out of the matchbox', simply because it reflects my life. I have always felt God must have given me a creative talent for a reason, and by stepping out in faith to use my creative skills for Him, God has brought my childhood dream of being an illustrator to life! Like the match being struck to bring light and warmth, I feel God has used my paintings to bring the light of the gospel to others!

Let Him use you and trust that He has a plan for your life to bring hope and a future! (Jeremiah 29:11)

Izzy Watson

1
God's human email

Esther 4 v 6-17

"Esther sent Hathak to Mordecai in the open square to find out what was troubling him" . . . "Hathak went back and reported to Esther what Mordecai had said" . . . "then she instructed Hathak to go back and say to Mordecai" . . . "when Esther's words were reported to Mordecai he sent Hathak back with an answer . . ."

The book of Esther is a true Hollywood epic. It tells the story of the deliverance of the Jewish people from extermination.

I must confess to only recently coming across a character in the book of Esther named Hathak. Whether he was a believer in Esther's God we don't know, but God used him to facilitate critical messages between Mordecai and Esther. The problem was that Mordecai was outside the Palace and Esther was inside – they urgently needed to talk about the real threat of the potential ethnic cleansing of the Jews, supported by the wicked Haman.

No email, no facebook, no fax, no phone, no mobile, just a walking, talking 'human email' called Hathak.

I wonder if you find yourself in a place where you are sharing, administrating, organising, or delivering confidential instructions between people or leaders, but are somewhat invisible yourself. Without you, information goes astray or is not passed on, and practical issues are not resolved. You make sure it all goes smoothly and you see the results of all of your patient service, but perhaps it isn't recognised by others. We all relate to you!

Hathak gives us a picture of faithfulness and reliability. In many ways, leaders long to have teams of "Hathak staff".

Do you sometimes struggle to give thanks to God for the behind the scenes service he has entrusted you to do? Do you look with envy at those on a stage? We have all been tempted to fall for that! You are not alone.

Enjoy the person God has made you to be and remember, God is watching, and he will reward you on that day.

Let us give thanks to God for every opportunity to serve, including being a God anointed, 'human email' if that is where we find ourselves at a "time such as this" (Esther 4:14).

2
People before pigs

Mark 5 v 1-17

A demon possessed man is addicted to self-harm. Jesus meets him and casts the demons out into 2,000 pigs, who rush down the mountainside and drown. When the pig farmers come to Jesus (their business is in ruins), they see that the man, who had previously been possessed, was now completely different – he was properly dressed and relaxed! The farmers were afraid, and they began to plead with Jesus to leave that region. *(Summary)*

The well-being of people is often sacrificed at the mercy of big businesses. I have worked in the business world for many years and am acutely aware that profit so often comes before people.

In the bible, we read many miracles of healing done by Jesus. We are often captivated by the mercy shown to the individual. However, Jesus also uses miracles to expose hate-filled hearts in those who cannot celebrate from the heart, what has happened. Sadly, this is reflected in the pig farmers attitudes towards the healing of the demonised man. They did not celebrate the fact the demonised man had been healed, instead their hearts were full of fear, to the extent that they were desperate for Jesus to leave them.

Why were they full of fear?

"Jesus, 2000 pigs are dead. You are so irresponsible! We had an order for hundreds of bacon sandwiches but now our competition down the road will get the order as we can't deliver it. Couldn't you have sent the demons to a more convenient place?"

For Jesus, people came before profit.
For the pig farmers, profit came before people.

I shared this with a Christian company director and we asked ourselves "how would we have responded if we were those farmers?" In all honesty, we really weren't sure! Ouch . . . We realised that a business can indeed gloriously serve God, but would we be willing to see it destroyed for one man's life? We felt challenged to re-centre life in Christ and hold on to everything lightly.

3
Risky Love

Luke 10 v 35

'The next day he took out two denarii and gave them to the innkeeper. 'Look after him,' he said, 'and when I return, I will reimburse you for any extra expense you may have.'

Recently, I'd heard of a man who had seen a young person stranded on a motorway after a breakdown. He saw the potential danger he was in, and ran onto the motorway to bring them to the hard shoulder to safety. Unfortunately, a driver didn't see the rescuer and struck him with their vehicle. He died. The young person who had broken down survived without injury. Love is instinctive and risky.

We are all familiar with the general theme of the Good Samaritan. The least likely, 'non-religious' person, comes to the aid of a man described as 'half dead' on the road, whilst 'religious' people walk on by. They are too busy to get their hands dirty.

I was pondering this parable recently and noticed something afresh.

The Samaritan not only provided the two denarii but also put himself at financial risk. He says that he will "pick up the bill for any extra expense". The Samaritan knows nothing of the character of the injured man. Supposing after he has been left to rest, the 'injured' man decides to stay another week at the inn. The inn becomes "the Holiday Inn". He might raid the mini-bar in his room for spirits and ask for a new set of clothes! He will reassure the innkeeper that his guarantor will pay the final bill in full. The bible doesn't tell us that he took advantage of his stay, but that isn't the focus. The focus is how lavish the love of the Samaritan was. The Good Samaritan will see the bill and is committed to paying up. He puts himself at a degree of risk for a stranger.

Risky love is not usually seen by others but only by God. I guess that's authenticity. Let's keep loving others even though it may be risky at times.

4

It Ripples Further than We Think

Jonah 1 v 5

'to lighten the load they threw the cargo overboard.'

We live in a radically independent culture which assumes we make good and bad choices in our private world without impact on others.

Jonah made a bad choice. He chose to run from God. We know he ended up inside a whale and got back on track in the end.

Within the text, Jonah jumps on board a ship in his attempt to run from God. God therefore sent a storm, in order to dissuade Jonah. In their fear, the other sailors onboard the vessel threw cargo overboard to try and steady the ship.

Here is the point. The cargo was now at the bottom of the ocean and was likely to contain large packed volumes of grain, which had been intended for the markets to feed families, therefore it would have been valuable. Historians have also noted the ancient trade route.

Jonah's 'private' sin caused pain for himself in the belly of a whale, the storm terrified the sailors, and the people who needed the cargo were also at a loss.

5

Jumping the barbed wire fences

Galatians 6 v 1

"Brothers and sisters, if someone is caught in a sin, you who live by the Spirit, should restore that person gently"

As a child, I was often taken by my parents to walk in England's New Forest. I routinely loved the challenge of jumping over fences laden with barbed wire whilst I happily ignored shouts of, "use the turnstile Jonathan!" behind me. "A far more boring way to progress the walk", I thought.

Often my timing wasn't perfect and I would get stuck on the fence, held firmly in place by the barbed wire. My woolly jumper, jeans and socks would be caught on the barbs intended to warn wandering livestock rather than enthusiastic kids.Invariably, I would find that I had scraped or cut myself and the more I moved to struggle free from the barbs, the clothes would tear, and the cuts get worst. Hence, a shout of, "help me I'm stuck!!" would ring out.

Christians on 'the barbs'

God loves his people. He wants them to enjoy him now and forever.

Still, there are so many 'barbs' that we can be caught on, and the variety is endless. Over-consumption of food or alcohol, pride, addiction . . ., and the list goes on.

The challenge to the church is to invest time in people who find themselves 'caught', but are shouting "help". In humility, we also need to examine our own lives:

1. We cannot help a christian until they ask for it.

2. Once they shout "help" we approach them in gentle love, affirming our own weakness, in order to reveal that they are not alone.

3. We need a culture of journeying with each other in openess, whereby we walk in the light with someone. I think unfortunately, this is a rarity, and that is why Satan fights to keep your problem secret.

Let's help people to come off the barbed wire fence in gentleness and walk in the light with each other.

6
Thinking on your feet

Luke 12:12

'When you are brought before the synagogues, rulers, and authorities, do not worry about how to defend yourselves or what to say, for at that time the Holy Spirit will teach you what you should say.'

I recall a time in Switzerland when I was at a business meeting in a major city. The meeting had been called as a very large project was emerging which my company could win. After the meeting, we all went to eat together in a restaurant and the wine was flowing amongst the 12. I kept myself sober, but was aware that I 'stuck out' from the crowd. Around 11.55pm, as the meal was drawing to a close, I seemed to sense a very clear prompt from the Lord. It was along the lines of, "in 5 minutes the people you are with will want to go to a place that I don't want you to go – you need to walk away immediately." I realised this would mean walking away from my job responsibility to look after our client, the major company.

As we stood outside the restaurant, sure enough they decided that they wanted to go to a club where there could be substantial conflict with my faith. I politely said that I couldn't attend, and walked away. I chose to escape a situation where people were already high on alcohol. Escaping without discussion is sometimes right.

I walked away into the night politely and realised that I had not only walked away from my job, but I also couldn't recall where the hotel was!

As I walked, I saw a man on the street and mentioned the name of the hotel, he said nothing but pointed the way. I turned the corner and the hotel appeared right in front of me! It seemed that the time required to return to the hotel was much faster than walking to the restaurant. I don't know if I had met an angel.

In the morning I asked how the evening went. The nightclub had been a very bad experience and apparently they were glad to leave.

We need to remember that God is with us wherever we go and he will be faithful to his children at their time of need.

7
Routine Interruption

Acts 10 v 3

'One day at about three in the afternoon he had a vision. He distinctly saw an angel of God who came to him and said "Cornelius!"

What is your 3 o'clock in the afternoon? Think back to a time when you were suddenly interrupted by a call which turned out to be very important, it could have been in the middle of the night, morning, evening or 3pm in the afternoon.

There are times in our lives when we pray good prayers that make Jesus smile. That's a good thing! Only one problem. We are sometimes surprised by the answer God gives. It can indeed be a 'rude' interruption.

I often use the facilities of a coffee shop in the centre of town where I tap away on my laptop. I sometimes pray, "Lord if you want to interrupt me at any time to serve you, please do . . ."

One day about 1pm a handicapped man (who I knew) approached me on his motorised scooter. We greeted each other and then he showed me the state of his nails . . . they had grown very long. He said, "Jon, these nails have grown so long and it's painful because I catch them on things." Confused I replied, "you have a carer – why doesn't she cut them?""She can't cut them as it's against the Government's health and safety regulations."

A nudge came from God at that point, "do something about it." He stayed in the café whilst I found a manicure shop and the next thing I knew, my friend found his hands soaking in warm water and 15 mins later after cutting, relieved from pain.

As I ponder this, I realise that my understanding of serving God is still distorted. The attraction of some public ministry is very strong. That's where the applause of men is loudest. It has taken a while for me to see that the Lord smiles when I obey in simplicity rather than looking for the big things.

In the text, Cornelius is engaged in everyday life before an Angel appears. The key for all of us is that doing simple acts of love makes God smile. In his case, God noted Cornelius' prayers and gifts to the poor. This routine of faithful service qualified Cornelius to receive a visitation from God.

Let's be faithful in the routines, and let God deliver our 3pm interruption!

8
Fishing for Cash

Matthew 17 v 27

"Go to the lake and catch the first fish you see, you will find a '4 Drachma coin' to pay for your tax and mine"

Peter is expected to pay the temple tax in keeping with Jewish tradition. He doesn't have the money handy in his pocket and so he turns to Jesus for help. The easy and straight forward approach would be for Jesus to use cash resources to solve the problem. However, Jesus sees an opportunity to use the situation to help Peter grow. The idea that the money can be sourced from the mouth of a fish, is so bizarre and comical that it must have stunned Peter.

Jesus was testing the extent to which Peter trusted him. It made no sense. The question is whether he would trust him anyway. Peter passes the test and goes fishing. The first fish he catches had the coin in its mouth.

Jesus already knew when that first fish would swim by with a coin in its mouth, in preparation for it to be caught by Peter.

The key lesson for Peter was:

"Peter I know you are worried about finding the money to pay the temple tax. Rather than just giving you the cash, I wanted you to gain a revelation that I am God and I know all of the faintest movements within all of creation. I know when a rain drop will fall to the ground and I know the movements of all of the fish in the sea, and thus, which one carried a coin in its mouth at the very time you went fishing. Don't worry Peter, trust me; I am God and have an all seeing eye which has no limits. This experience will strengthen your faith"

Whatever your need, be aware that God may take you on a "fishy" route to help you grow in the knowledge of who he is, as well as supply all of your needs.

9
Money is Neutral

2 Corinthians 9 v 11

"You will be enriched in every way so that you can be generous on every occasion"

Money is neutral . . . it's made of paper or coins. However . . . whilst money is neutral, it does take on the character of the one who possesses it. God does not mind us having money. He does mind money having us.

I felt God speaking to me about this recently using the illustration of money being like rain falling from heaven on two kinds of hearts.

Pond heart

The rain falls on the pond and it collects and builds. The water is good to drink from for a couple of days, but after three months it is already poisonous. This represents the prosperity gospel at its worst. The problem being that there is no outward flow of blessing to others.

River heart

The rain falls on to a river. Always drinkable, always flowing to where the Spirit leads it to go. This person recognises he is a steward of what God owns. This person often sees God's provision of money increasing, which becomes larger as God trusts him more to handle wealth.

So the question is "do we give to get?"

No, we cannot manipulate God like this. However, I have often found that over the years God rewards me financially when I am least expecting it. God always seems to make sure that it is a complete surprise to me – a sudden blessing.

You attract God's attention when he is looking to trust someone with a task for the kingdom. When you give to others financially, you launch a kingdom world far beyond what you can imagine. You get God's attention and attract his favour.

Enjoy your joyful giving!

10
A Bridge too far

Psalm 51 v 10

"Create in me a clean heart and renew a steadfast spirit in me."

Coaches are often unable to cross over a bridge as the weight would damage the bridge or indeed cause a total collapse. These visual warning signs are provided on the road before a bridge, and come in different weight bearing levels, according to the designed strength of the bridge.

When I was asking the lord at the beginning of the year to share his goal for my life, he said one thing.

Grow a steadfast and godly character.

For Christians the word steadfast is defined as, 'a consistency of Godly responses, especially use of words, within life and an unwavering focus on God within a circumstantial storm or indeed a time of blessing'. Steadfast people are not easily shaken. I must confess that I am aware of needing to grow in this!

A very close business friend, a christian who I had known for over 25 years, wrote me a letter with multiple things he thought were wrong with me and the reason he couldn't work with me anymore. Painful and perplexed, I sought to get together in person with him to chat through the letter over coffee. But he said there was no need, and promptly blocked my number. My attempt for godly reconciliation was rejected. Now, I had two choices, bitterness, or handing my friend wholly over into God's hands, trusting and knowing I had tried to do the right thing in forgiving him. It was painful, but I know God was building a steadfast life in me.

Back to bridges. Why then is a steadfast character so important?

It is a leadership issue. God intends us to grow in a steadfast spirit so that we can carry the "weight" of more people in the "coaches of life" and all of their challenging situations. God wants people to see our character grow in depth. The stronger our spiritual bridges, the more responsibility God will give us as he knows we can handle it.

Bridge building is not glamorous and often happens in dark places where through one Godly choice after another we grow. Let's take courage and grow in steadfastness.

11
Petrol pumps for Jesus

Proverbs 11:25

"A generous person will prosper. He who refreshes others will himself be refreshed."

If a petrol pump was human, it wouldn't be a glamorous lifestyle. Cars drive in and grab the pump, pay, and go.

I wonder what God sees as eye catching? Public gifts of teaching, singing, preaching and the like are important, but only a few can do them.

The ministry of the petrol pump allows people to refuel and then get back to serving God in many ways. The 'vehicle of ministry' once again drives with a full tank and now the focus of recognition is on the driver's ministry, not the pump.

The text says that a generous person will prosper and that he who refreshes others will himself be refreshed.

Here is the key question. When people drive to your pump, what kind of "fuel" do they find?

Encouragement or a cold shoulder, empathy or distance, a listener or one who answers before listening. Are you one who gives secretly when a financial need is clarified?

Do you find yourself enjoying the ministry of the petrol pump as a lifestyle, perhaps only being seen by God? If you do, you will enjoy being refreshed at surprising times!

12

Photoshopping Jesus out of culture

John 8:31-32

"If you hold on to my truth, you are really my disciples. Then you will know the truth and the truth will set you free."

Photoshopping is the use of editing software for electronic images, the most common of which are of people. The software enables manipulation, smoothing out unwanted blemishes, resizing and colour adjustment. Typically it enables people to look stronger or more beautiful or more presentable than in real life.

"Have we photoshopped Jesus in our lives?" In other words, have we altered Jesus' truths in order to suit our own lives/cultures? In the text we see that holding on to the truth and the teachings of Christ is the foundation for knowing the truth and walking in freedom as a disciple of Jesus.

Jesus called us to be his disciples. 'Photoshopped Christianity' calls us to be religious consumers of services and please cultural ideals. The challenge is to have an awareness that the culture we live in can transform us into its image, rather than following Jesus. If we follow Him we can be transformed into His image and therefore rely wholly on God, whilst loving and spreading the good news to others.

How can we avoid being photoshopped into the image of culture rather than holding onto the truth and being ambassadors of Christ?

There are many areas. But perhaps a deep humility before God and awareness of his greatness is the most important. When we are not satisfied to serve God as a lifestyle, we are photoshopped into prevailing culture.

Humbling ourselves before God protects us from a key word. Deception. Humility protects us also from being 'Pharisee-like' and seeking to point out the faults of a culture with no sense of grace and merely point scoring.

Let's allow the Holy Spirit to shine on areas of our lives where Jesus and his truths have been photoshopped out, so we can live as full disciples of Christ.

13

Start Well Finish Well

Nehemiah 3 v 1

"Eliashib the high priest and his fellow priests went to work and rebuilt the sheep gate."

Nehemiah 13 v 4

"Eliashib the priest had been put in charge of the storerooms of the house of God. He was closely associated with Tobiah and he had provided him with a large room formerly used to store the grain offerings, incense and temple articles, tithes of grain . . ."

Your life journey is not so much how you start but how you finish.

In the book of Nehemiah, the walls are broken and Eliashib the high priest starts the work rebuilding the sheep gate. This gate allowed the lambs to be brought through for sacrifice for sin. Eliashib means "God provides" in Hebrew. The picture of Jesus as the lamb of God is clear.

It all started well.

But Tobiah, an enemy of God, had befriended Eliashib after the walls were rebuilt in chapter 13. He managed to persuade Eliashib to hire a spare room in the house of God which was normally filled with temple articles, incense and more.

Eliashib was in charge of the storehouse. Tobiah was an opportunist and he took advantage of this. Tobiah had actually mocked the rebuilding work publicly saying that a fox climbing on the wall would break it down. Eliashib would have known this. He is described as being closely associated with Tobiah. This seems incredible!

Satan is indeed an opportunist.

The challenge for us is to stay alert. Be wise. Don't let the enemy in through the backdoor.

No wonder Nehemiah threw Tobiah's pots and pans out onto the streets when he found out! (Nehemiah 13 v 8)

14
Unexpected healing

2 Kings 5 v 10, 11

'Elisha sent a messenger to say, "Go wash yourself seven times in the Jordan, and your flesh will be restored and you will be cleansed" ... "I thought that he would surely come to me and call on the name of his God, wave his hand over the skin and cure me ... aren't the rivers of Damascus better that the Jordan?"

I suffered for 5 years with psoriasis on one of my lower legs and foot but it only affected one leg not the other. Psoriasis has the appearance of patchy skin and redness. I sought out steroid treatments from the doctor and used this for 3 years, however it only had the effect of reducing itching. It didn't bring healing.

I generally eat well, but prayerfully decided to further improve my overall health as a general principle. I switched to routinely eating fresh tuna and salmon, walnuts, blueberries and avocado. I continued this purely for general health reasons. A month later I noticed my skin was completely healed.

The situation that Naaman found himself in was similar because he was expecting supernatural prayer to be the source for healing. The idea that the river Jordan would be the place of healing seemed ridiculous, especially as it was much dirtier compared to better known rivers. However, he went into the Jordan in obedience to the specific command and was healed.

Taking the illustration further, let's ponder the offence of Naaman. He is thinking naturally when he says aren't the rivers of Damascus better than the Jordan? I myself was thinking, "surely the steroids are better than simple foods." I was really saying, "surely what God has provided is no match for modern medicines." How wrong I was! How wrong Naaman was. He thought that the clean medical properties of river Damascus were better.

So for me, medicine was good but not the answer. I wonder if we have missed other sources of healing for other areas in our lives?

Let's be ready to see God's solution!

15
Oxygen of Comfort

2 Cor 1 v 3-4

"Praise be the God and father of our Lord Jesus Christ, the father of compassion and the God of all comfort who comforts us in all our troubles so that we can comfort those in any trouble with comfort we ourselves have received from God."

The word 'comfort' in biblical language and culture, was used when the roman soldiers were going into battle. Comfort was used in the context of giving strength and support to the soldier in front to keep them from falling, thus the soldiers moved forward as a team unit. The soldier giving strength needs to be strong enough himself to complete this task.

So what does this comfort or strength look like for us.

We all listen to the safety announcements before a plane takes off.

One key instruction is to place the oxygen mask on yourself before attempting to help the child next to you with their mask. We need to have sufficient oxygen in our lungs to be strong enough in ourselves to help the person next to us. We have to receive God's love and strength before we can help others.

I need to draw on God as a lifestyle to have the capacity to serve others when God calls.

How are you doing with breathing in the comfort of God so that you can serve others with that comfort? Make time alone with God and ask him to show you who needs comforting.

16
What's in a name?

Luke 19 v 8

In the words of Zacchaeus: "If I have cheated anybody out of anything, I will pay back four times the amount."

Humans can be corrupted. Zacchaeus was a tax inspector. The trouble was, he used his position to take extra taxes all for himself. His pockets were full of bonus cash.

The name 'Zacchaeus' actually means 'uncorrupted' or 'pure'. In Jewish culture, names were very important. Parents chose a name with the best of intentions, therefore Zacchaeus' parents hoped he would be known for a great character. But his 'bonus tax' collection strategy destroyed that reputation.

After meeting Jesus, he comes to a realisation that his life needed to change.

The encounter meant that Zacchaeus was also given a new 'name' confirming his new identity – "son of Abraham". This declared to the Jews that he now belonged to God. Jesus was saying, "Your parents wanted you to be known as a man of integrity. Now I have put my seal on your life. Even the name Zacchaeus is not good enough for you." 'Son of Abraham' confirms your identity as MY SON.

Just imagine the scene at downtown Jericho street: –

Zacchaeus: "Knock knock."

Tenant: "Who's there."

Zacchaeus: "Zacchaeus."

Tenant: "Not you again. I've given you the extra taxes already this month!"

Zacchaeus "I've come to say sorry. I was wrong and selfish to get extra taxes from you. Here – let me give you back four times what I took. I met this man Jesus and it changed everything. Please take the money – I was wrong.

Tenant: Could you tell me more about Jesus? This change in your life is amazing. Come in and BE A GUEST AT MY HOME. I want to know more. Tea or coffee?

Can you imagine the hundreds that would have heard the life changing power of Zacchaeus meeting Jesus and thus turned to Christ themselves?

Are you seeking to reach one person with the gospel who you know has a bad reputation? Don't underestimate the power of gospel to reach that one person who will be given a new name, a child of God, which will impact hundreds.

17

Standing out from the crowd

2 Timothy 2:19

"The Lord knows those who are his"

When my father died, we were left with his very impressive collection of British and foreign coins. Some 500 coins in all. My mother asked me to have the coins valued, so I took them to a well known valuer in London.

The weight of the folders was significant. Each coin had been carefully placed in a transparent pocket and with some 50 pockets per presentation, it was easy for the valuer to flick through and inspect at speed.

In anticipation, I watched the eye of the valuer go though the collection. He was very fast and knew what he was looking for. Unfortunately, neither the bronze or silver coins seemed to grab his attention until he suddenly swooped in on a small set of silver coins from a previous century.

He carefully removed them from their pockets and called to his director. "Can you come and see this."

The director came out and checked that they were genuine under his examination. "Genuine and a set of 4!"

An offer was made which my mother accepted.

The remaining bulk of coins had limited value. However the trained eye of the valuers could see what stood out.

God sees his children in the world as they stand out from the crowd. This is our encouragement as we live amongst people who do not have a love of Jesus.

18
Hold onto your Donkey lightly

Luke 19 v 33

"As they were untying the donkey, the owners asked them "why are you untying the donkey?" They replied "the Lord needs it."

Recently I heard a sermon informing me that our generosity towards God is only a response to the generosity of God towards us. This is so true. If God has given his only son to die for us and set us free, anything that we offer to him in return is an act of grateful worship.

We believe that everything on this planet belongs to God. Our houses, cars, food in the fridge, the casinos of Vegas, the oxygen I breathe. We have it on loan . . .

Lets just imagine the scene in Luke 19:

The disciples, under the command of Jesus, have the responsibility to fetch a donkey, however they are not even told to ask for permission. Let's tune in to what the disciples might have said as they go to fetch the goods.

"Hey mate. I was just thinking. What if the donkey owners say no! They might say 'who are you and what gives you the right to take our property?' What do we do if there is a fight. Should we call down fire from heaven?"

The disciples could only step into the command from Jesus and they did.

The response of the owners also challenges us. Their hearts were in the right place as they gave the donkey to the disciples. God had prepared their hearts because they were willing to hold on lightly to their stuff.

Are we ready to hand over our own 'donkeys'?

I wonder if I would. The nudges from the Holy Spirit are real and that thought to pass on something we own or money we have is so often a divine thought.

I need to walk with God holding my stuff lightly before him as if it is all his. We don't own our stuff, neither our lives, so let's give freely when the lord comes knocking on our door to receive what he owns.

19

Son conscious

Luke 15 v 20

"So he got up and went to his father, while he was still a long way off his father saw him and was filled with compassion for him. He ran to his son, threw his arms around him and kissed him."

The prodigal son had wasted away his entire inheritance, which he had demanded from his father before he went. As he comes back to his home, he expected to be rejected by his father. His father actually runs to him and throws his arms around him in love.

As Christians, we often miss the depth of the love of God. God wants us to stay close to him, yet we all fail in different ways. No exceptions. Sin means missing the mark. The mark is God's perfection. However, love wins!

We can capture the moment of reconciliation with a saying to remember.

"When I am SIN conscious, God is SON conscious. When I am SON conscious, SIN loses its appeal"

It's all about identity. Who are you?

What does it mean to be Son conscious?

Our heavenly father is actively running towards us not just when we get things right, but when we get things very wrong as well. Sonship speaks of security stability and peace.

Are we fully aware of our sonship? Ask God to reveal this truth to you today.

20
Checks and Balances

Isaiah 6 v 8

Then I heard the voice of the Lord saying "whom shall I send? Who will go for us?" And I said "here I am, send me!"

I was not a christian in 1986, but had been deeply challenged when I heard about the christian revival in South Korea. The outcome of this revival meant that the country now had 25% of the population following Jesus. I was reading a book by a South Korean pastor on prayer and I sought to copy him.

After many hours, at 11:30pm on December 17th 1986, I suddenly experienced an encounter with the Holy Spirit, so powerful that I knew Jesus was God. Instantly, I gasped "you are God – I want to live for you." I started to read the bible and my eyes were opened. I saw that He was true. I knew I had passed from death into a new life.

In the passage, it is clear that God knows Isaiah is ready to go anywhere.
Isaiah had already encountered God by seeing Him as He is, and receiving total cleansing from sin.

The challenge to myself and other Christians is that Isaiah volunteers and pleads with God to send him anywhere. Like Isaiah, I just want to obey. My encounter with God, meant that I knew He is who He says He is. There was no analysis. No checks and balances. I went out the following day and told everyone I had met Jesus.

Am I willing to encounter God afresh today such that I am thrilled to serve in any way? All I can say is yes I will do anything.

SEND ME!

21

Wisdom to 'melt the iceberg'

1 Kings 10 v 6

'The Queen of Sheba said to king Solomon "the report that I have heard in my country about your achievements and your wisdom is true."

Wisdom is many things, but I would say it's a supernatural way of getting from A to C without needing to go through B. Wisdom connects you faster to the right people. Wise people are solution providers to situations. When we receive God's wisdom we will find things happening around us that cannot be explained by any other way than God's hand at work!

Here's what is so important: Those who aren't Christians will see the wisdom in us and will wonder "where did this wisdom come from?" People will then ask us to solve problems. As with the Queen of Sheba, they will be amazed to find that "what they heard" was true when they see the results.

I sometimes feel that the church sometimes seeks to spread the gospel in a one dimensional way. Imagine an iceberg. The iceberg represents the hard resistance to the gospel. Imagine 10 people volleying tennis balls at the ice with all their might. Nothing happens. So we call another 100 church members to volley tennis balls. Nothing happens. So a mega church is phoned and 5000 turn up and they volley the balls with all their might at the iceberg. Nothing happens except the balls bounce back and knock out the volunteers! We need to stop and ask for wisdom.

Solomon influenced those in authority like the Queen of Sheba. We too can influence those in authority for God. But for most of us it will be influencing those around us within the rhythm of everyday life. The appreciation given to the cashier, the kind reaction in a potentially hostile situation.

Matthew 5 v 13 "You are the salt of the earth."

Salt was a preservative in ancient times and today is spread on icy roads to clear them. Imagine, a helicopter dropping tons of salt on an iceberg. Day after day, the helicopter delivers more salt to drop, however, there is no visible result. The salt is working but you cannot see it. One day the pilot flies over the iceberg only to find it has crashed into the sea.

Will you ask God for more wisdom today and be the 'influencer' in your area?

22
Soaring or sailing?

Matthew 16:25

"Anyone who wants to save his life will lose it. He who loses his life for me will find it"

A few years ago I met a young couple who had truly 'arrived at' or 'achieved' their dream. I met them by an Italian lake where they had rented out a small house which was their launching pad for their passion, which was windsurfing and sailing.

But this couple were super rich. They had been working in the city of London and had amassed a vast sum, which they projected would allow them to effectively do what they wanted for their life ahead. No more work. Just leisure and pleasure, enjoying cafés and wind surfing. This was highly unusual by UK standards and, like lottery winners, they were the picture-perfect couple who had got to a place where they knew money would come in whilst they lived an idealistic life.

When I first heard this, I felt that sense of "wow". I felt slightly embarrassed as one who, like most people, needed to work. I couldn't imagine being retired at their ages.

Then I pondered the bible. Following Jesus can indeed bring restful times of "sailing". However, the core value of following Jesus is based on service and sacrifice for a glory that lasts for eternity rather than this temporary life on earth.

Comfort zones are destroyed by the Lord. An adult eagle will begin to destroy the comfortable nest that baby eagles have grown in. Not to cause harm, but to make sure they soar, as they are forced to fly. A small first flight, a few more, and then soaring on the wind currents.

Soaring not sailing.

Let's reflect on the challenge of following Jesus. How am I doing?

Am I still following Jesus? Am I still taking risks of faith? How about you?

Let's soar.

23
Unity that wins the race

John 13:35

"By this shall all men know that you are my disciples, that you have love for one another"

In the Olympics there are many competitive sports including rowing in teams. Rowing in unity requires a "cox" at the front who will dictate the pace of the rowing and watch for perfect unity of the oars entering the water at the same time. The timing and combined effort will enable the boat to win the race by reaching the finishing line faster.

The cox is usually a light smaller person, often a young woman. Her call needs to be listened to by all of the men who will focus on her. The cox is also responsible for steering the boat and coordinating the power and rhythm of the rowers. Like the believers tuning into God himself, Spirit lead unity allows the church to display who he is to the world. The church portrays God's love and consequently non-believers wonder who this God is.

Our cox is the holy spirit who dwells within. We can attune our lives to the rhythm of his voice.

So we see the power of unity in the church. How do we deal with areas of disunity?

Unforgiveness is the great threat to unity. It starves the church of its power.

Are we holding any grudges against anyone in our church? If we do then our spiritual oars will be entering the water at different times robbing us of the great power of united love.

Let's win the race together listening the quiet voice of the Holy Spirit whispering "unite".

24

All your padlocks are open

Psalm 142 v 7

"Set me free from my prison that I may praise your name. Then the righteous will gather about me because of your goodness to me."

Baby elephants are chained by foot to the stage in a circus. However when they grow older they do not need the chain. Realistically, the adult elephant could walk off the stage, yet its mind still thinks the chain is there. It does not move.

The thinking of the baby elephant does not change into adulthood. Scripture says "It is for freedom. That Christ has set u free" Galatians 5 v 1. Many of us are still believing lies. Despite knowing Jesus, we can still live as if we are not redeemed.

The bible also says, "open the gates that the righteous nations may enter" Isaiah 26:2. There are so many gates that the Lord wants us to walk through. Gates of opportunity, gates of ministry, gates to new jobs, gates to know him deeper. Yet we so often don't walk through the gates of opportunity as our mind tells us there are 'padlocks' on the gates.

If we are walking by the Spirit, we can call on God and be confident that he is leading. We will not be threatened by gates that look padlocked but call on God to lead us forward with confidence.

What an interesting ending to the verse. "Then the righteous will gather about me because of your goodness to me." When we find freedom and see the gates open, those who also know Christ are drawn like a magnet, as they too are attracted to Him. They see the freedom on us and know God's presence is there.

25
Bending the truth

Exodus 32 v 1-3

'When the people saw that Moses was so long coming down from the mountain, they gathered around Aaron and said, "Come, make us gods who will go before us. We don't know what has happened to Moses." All the people took off their earrings and brought them to Aaron. He took what they handed him and made them into an idol, cast in the shape of a calf, fashioning it with a tool. They said "these are your real Gods Israel, who brought you up out of Egypt" . . . they engaged in eating, drinking, and immorality.'

v 24

'I told them "whoever has any gold jewellery, take it off." Then they gave me the gold, and I threw it into the fire and out came this calf!'

It is such a temptation to bend the truth. We shape things to protect ourselves. How often I find this a challenge! When we are caught doing something wrong, we will shift the blame to divert responsibility. But the main reason we lie is fear. We are afraid of the consequences.

I was re-reading the familiar story of the golden calf. Moses is away from the camp for 40 days. We know that Aaron actually cast the molten gold into the shape of a calf. Hardly a quick job but one that required focus and determination. A clear choice. The people had been recently freed from Egypt where they had numerous gods, therefore an animal god was a comfort zone of familiarity. But it wasn't just bending the gold, it was bending the truth that Aaron fell into. Aaron stated to Moses that "he threw the jewellery straight in the fire," shifting the blame onto the people. Rather than admitting his error clearly, he seems to suggest that the calf just appears! – it lead the people into syncretistic mixed worship of God. This lead to the whole community being corrupted.

If we are not careful, we can do the same. Imagine interviews with Police:
"I didn't see the one way road sign!"
"I was listening to music and didn't realise I was driving at nearly 100 miles/hr!"

How do we get the 'Aaron' out of us?

Ask for help from a trusted friend or leader to give honest feedback on whether you bend the truth sometimes. I do this for myself.

26
Sticker embarrassment

Ephesians 4:15

"Instead speaking the truth in love, we will grow to become more like Christ."

When I was in my early twenties, I sometimes supported youth groups and youth conferences. At one conference, we were asked to put on a sticker to identify us. My sticker read "my name is Jon" together with a big smile.

The conference was fun and finished at around 4pm. I walked home and, en route, began to pick up items from a major supermarket, news agent and chemist. All very normal. But I had forgotten to take off the badge. I was aware that I was receiving quite a few smiles as I paid for goods at the tills. Perhaps a "holy awe" from the conference was over me I thought!

Eventually, I dropped in at my friends house who asked me how things had gone. "The big sticker is eye catching." He said pointing at me. I stared down in shock and took it off with a sense of relief.

Suddenly my memory rushed back through all the shops I had been to, and the smiles I had received. How embarrassing! Very humbling.

There is a serious point here. Whilst the many were smiling at me, they said nothing. My friend was the one who pointed out that I needed to remove it.

In life, we cannot see the things that others do. Especially in the church. But the text from Ephesians urges us to "speak the truth in love." If we really understand biblical love, we will graciously approach others where we need to point something out.

We all need to change and hear the truth.

We can see it. They can't. So our motive for helping them "in love" is to serve and help them grow.
Let's help each other remove our badges.

27

Overcoming the valleys of life

1 kings 20:23

"The Arameans think that the Lord is a God of the hills and not of the valleys."

After finishing university, I went with a friend on a trek down the Grand Canyon. At the top of the Canyon, people were eating ice-cream, drinking coffee and feeling at ease whilst gazing at the view. However, walking down the canyon you were aware of being away from everything except a few lizards. We desired our ice-creams the further we walked. Life is a mixture of seasons and experiences. Sometimes we are enjoying the ice-cream of life 'on the hills' and sometimes we are facing tougher times 'in the valleys'.

The Arameans believed that the reason they lost a battle was because of its physical location. That battle was fought on a hill, therefore they lured Israel into a deeper valley, believing they would win the next fight. The Arameans believed God's protection over his people in Israel was limited by physical demographics. They were mistaken. In the valley, Israel won again.

We need to trust and know that God is near his people wherever they are. It's easy to believe that when life is in "ice-cream" mode, it is much harder when life becomes very challenging.

Christians are not immune from problems. Jesus actually promised that "in this world, you will have trouble" (John 16:33) – my friends and I are currently facing challenges such as divorce, unemployment, illness, loneliness and . . . the list goes on. These are the valley experiences. There is warfare for the Christian, usually not against a physical army, rather an invisible enemy. Satan is more likely to whisper at an opportune time when you're down in the 'valley', rather than 'eating ice-creams' on the hills. Our minds and the world can come into an unconscious agreement with Satan. Before we know it, we have lost touch with God's promises.

Are you walking through valleys at the moment? We need to acknowledge that our pain is real and give it to God, who knows, loves and cares for us. We can also recall the good things God is doing in our lives during tough times. "The God of all grace who called you to his eternal glory in Christ, after you have suffered a little while, will himself restore you and make you strong, firm and steadfast." (1 Peter 5:10)

28
Roaring confidence

Proverbs 28 vs 1

"The wicked flee though no-one pursues but the righteous are as bold as a lion"

I recall the many times I have driven down motorways and felt frustrated at the signs indicating a maximum speed limit change from 70 to 50 when there appears little reason for it. Sometimes I will see other cars drive at over 60 overtaking me and then I assume it is ok to follow.

Then I see a police car just ahead or worse, in my rear view mirror and my conscience is alerted. I slow down. I don't want him to catch me! But conscience then says "why were you not just obeying the signs in front of you in the first place?" I don't want to be fearful of seeing flashing lights pursuing me in my mirror! A word of confession goes forth and forgiveness is received.

What helps us walk in boldness like a lion? Recently I've see how vital clear vision enables boldness. A lion waits in preparation for the moment to "go" and when he does his vision is clear. Scripture says "my people perish for lack of vision," but it's those who are righteous in Christ who see vision. When vision is clear we move. We are not checking our 'rear view mirrors'.

Now you might say "who are the wicked?"

Christians also make bad choices right? We sin every day. But the wicked are fundamentally against the work of Christ. They don't see the need to repent.

The righteous are like a compass that always returns to due north as the natural resting place reaching upwards to heaven. The wicked default to a random compass setting which is like a rudderless boat.

Our conscience is God given and precious indeed. Hebrews 10:22 says that our hearts our cleansed to relieve us from a guilty conscience. It all went wrong when Adam hid in the garden from God when he heard "where are you Adam?" Sin makes us hide but the blood of Jesus cleanses.

Call on Jesus and make him Lord. He will fill you with vision. Your compass will return to due North. Be as bold as a lion.

29

Flourishing in the presence of evil

Psalm 52 v 8

"I am like an olive tree flourishing in the house of God."

Some years ago I was driving through the olive groves of California. Huge crops were harvested and sold along the way in numbers of mini-supermarkets. Eating a freshly picked olive was indeed delicious. The atmosphere was serene, peaceful and tranquil.

There are things in life that are anything but tranquil that cause me to rise in anger and demand justice. It includes the horrors of murder around the world, the robbing of the elderly, or the crushing of the poor in the presence of the rich. My heart usually wants immediate justice and I want to take the situation and fix it myself, which in most cases, is of course impossible. I become distracted from God. I can become unsettled in myself as if God was not aware of the situation.

David says he is like a flourishing olive tree. Perhaps in Israel he recalled times of finding himself in a series of olive groves enjoying an occasional purchase from the local markets. However the atmosphere was anything but serene, he was aware that an enemy, an Edomite called Doeg, had done great evil. David knew this man had killed many of his people, including an entire village. (1 Samuel 22:18-19) As he was on the run and in danger himself, David had to hand over the frustration that he was now powerless and couldn't inflict justice himself.

So how did David deal with the "if only" questions.
David, being on the run, could only turn to the Lord. He declares that turning to God brings flourishing in the midst of such evil. Today some of the olive trees of Israel have been there for 2000 years. Still flourishing and bearing fruit over such a long time, rooted in God's soil.

David aligns himself with the longevity of the Olive tree. But the special olive tree he aligns himself to, is one flourishing in the house of God.

It is so hard to turn to God rather than make justice happen in our own strength. But ultimately, resting in God to complete his own justice is the only way.

30
Keep an eye on the fire

Romans 12:11

"Never be lacking in zeal but keep your spiritual fervour serving the Lord"

My parents have a fireplace in their home. When I lived there as a youngster I often had the role of building the fire for the evening. The fire was made of 'small kindling wood' (balls of paper and very small pieces of coal) which I arranged carefully in a pyramid shape and when ready, lit the paper. I watched to see that the fire was beginning to develop, then I arranged larger pieces of coal around the fire. Once the large pieces were assembled I assumed the basis for a roaring fire was in place for several hours.

Sometimes, however, I would take my eyes of the fire, watch TV and not notice that the fire had gone out. I hadn't kept watch to ensure the small fire developed properly to provide the required warmth for the whole room.
How did I lose the focus?
I had looked at the larger pieces of coal and had assumed that the small fire which I couldn't see now, was still ablaze. But it wasn't.

How do we know our fires have 'gone out'? In Revelation, we see the call to return to our first love (Revelation 3:20). A spiritual fire that has gone out is usually linked with self-reliant pride. Pride brings deception. You don't know when you've been deceived. You don't know when you've "gone out". To keep our fervour serving the Lord means keeping close to the source, Jesus, and walking in dependence on him not on our own 'performance'.

Are we aware of our lives being mechanical rather than "in-tune" with the Holy Spirit?
Are we humbling ourselves before God regularly?
Are we aware of God calling us to creative solutions given by the creator?
Let's keep the fire burning.

31
Incensed burning incense

2 Chronicles 26 v 16

"But after Uzziah became powerful, his pride led to his downfall. He was unfaithful and entered the temple of the Lord to burn incense on the altar. Azariah the priest with 80 other courageous priests of the Lord followed him in. They confronted King Uzziah and said 'it is not right for you Uzziah to burn incense to the Lord' . . . v 20 Uzziah became angry. While he was raging at the priests in their presence, leprosy broke out on his forehead.'

Uzziah and his father Amaziah had very promising Hebrew names meaning "My strength is Jehovah." His mother, Jekoliah, means "the perfection of the Lord." He started well, and he had a good mentor, Zecheriah to help him follow the Lord. God helped him in battle and gave him an entrepreneurial spirit in making better weaponry, indeed he became very powerful.

People let me know if I am good in one particular area of my life. I am blessed to hear that I am serving people well with this area. However the temptation is to daydream of a gift that is beyond what I have received and more out of step with the Holy Spirit.

Uzziah had done pretty much everything, but one opportunity had eluded him . . . to burn incense in the temple. I doubt that this priestly duty would have attracted him whilst building his empire, but once you have it all, the heart can reach for more. "Not only do I have all of this stuff, I am a man of the temple." But he was caught in the act by the priests and became furious. He had overstretched his anointing rather than resting in self-awareness. He was presumptuous.

Have you ever seen someone completely explode in a situation? A situation where that person is in the wrong? Many famous people have met their downfall through public denial with expressed anger only to find that evidence of wrong doing is confirmed.

Uzziah's anger was fearsome when he got caught, therefore God gives him leprosy. Why didn't he confess to God? Pride is terrible as it blinds you to knowing you are proud. He was incensed burning incense.

We need to watch our own hearts.

32
Rejected but Blessed

1 John 1 v 46

"Nazareth, can anything good come from there?" Nathanuel asked. "Come and see" said Philip.

If there had been on-line dating agencies in biblical days, you would have wanted to disguise your postal address if you lived in Nazareth. The "Jerusalem region" might have been a better choice to help your profile get more hits, "Nazareth" however, would have been less appealing! People living there would have been looking for road links to get out to a major city. It definitely wasn't a "city-break" location.

I recalled the day I was walking through my town centre shopping mall. It was one of those occasions when I felt I heard a voice of God speak to me in an inner voice. "Jon do you think anything good can come out of where you are living in?"

I said "I hope so" back to the Lord. In the text Philip has more faith than I. He said "come and see" –Philip was pointing to a person. Jesus.

Have you tried exchanging Nazareth for a place you know? How would you feel if that place turned out to be a great blessing.

33

Decreasing to look like Jesus

John 3:30

"he must increase, I must decrease"

Ephesians 5:27

"... to present her to himself as a radiant church, without stain or wrinkle or any other blemish but holy and blameless"

I have never enjoyed ironing thus I will gladly buy shirts that need less ironing. However, there are times when I know I have to look smart on the outside.

The shirt is eventually ready and is hung up to wear.

So how does the Lord mature the believer?

Firstly, consider a crumpled white shirt that is waiting to be ironed sitting at the bottom of a pile. Washed and dried but not ironed. Not ready to be worn.

So salvation in Christ makes us all clean. But transformation into Christ-likeness means submitting our lives to the "iron of the Lord" – so we not only smell right (justified before God) but are increasingly being transformed looking more and more like Christ as the creases are smoothed out. John 3:30 "He must increase – I must decrease" ... by de-creasing those shirts.

But God wants to present us to a world devoid of grace with a transformed life.

So will we allow God to change our lives to look more like him.

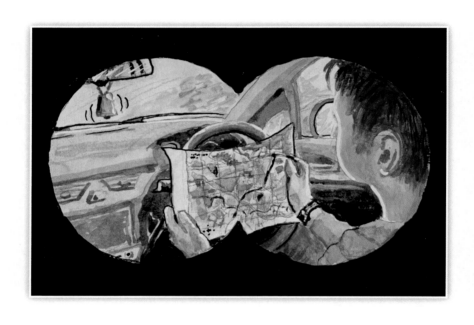

34
Your "Cowbell" is ringing in heaven

Psalm 34:15

The eyes of the Lord are on the righteous and his ears are attentive to their cry.

Recently I was in Switzerland and bought a cowbell.

Traditionally, a cowbell is used to ensure that the keeper of the cows could locate a wandering animal drawn away by the temptation of better grass or other distractions.

There are many valleys and mountains in Switzerland and it is too easy for cows to disappear down a ravine or behind a hill. Not visible to the keeper, the noise of the bell identifies the location of the lost animal.

For those who follow Jesus, we have a cowbell in our hearts called the Holy Spirit. Sometimes in life we feel that we are lost and that God doesn't see our situation. However, Psalm 34:15 assures us that the Lord both sees and hears us when we stray. When we feel lost or confused, the Holy Spirit within the believer 'rings' out to heaven. We are never out of sight.

If you do feel lost right now are you aware of drifting away from the body of Christ. Do you have a small group of close accountability to keep you focused.

35
Coffee distraction

Nehemiah 6 v 2,3

"Sanballat and Geshem sent me this message: Come, let us meet together in one of the villages on the plain of Ono."

(Nehemiah replied) "I am carrying on a great project and cannot go down. Why should the work stop while I leave it and go down to you?"

Some time ago I applied to go on a high profile conference in London on the theme of Business and the mission of God. I sent my application in and much to my surprise I received a call from the organiser who wanted to know more about my heart for the subject. He had been praying about the speakers. He then asked if I could be one! This was a great privilege and I accepted.

I completed my presentation and sat in a coffee shop near the conference venue ready for the main event. I knew God had given me a message for the meeting. I felt God's confidence. As I refreshed my memory on the notes, a smartly dressed lady appeared out of nowhere, sat down at my table, and began to speak to me. She said, "You don't know me but I need your help!" I replied, "In what way?" "I'm divorcing my husband and I need to be taken to a middle-eastern embassy to collect some documents." I said "I can't as I'm speaking at a conference. I can put you in a taxi?" She replied "No you must come!""No I cannot." She got up and left.

The other people in the café said to me, "what was that about?" I said "I think I know but you might not understand!"

I spoke at the conference and there was a wonderful sense of the power of God on me when I spoke. The feedback was wonderful. I was approached after speaking and asked to talk in other conferences! God had moved. No wonder the crafty attack.

I realise that Satan had presented a very plausible need and he knew I had a compassionate heart. Like the approach against Nehemiah, it was a strategy to delay the work. But discernment is key for all of us.

So who was the woman? I think she was a vulnerable person whom the enemy sought to use. Satan is an opportunist. We need to follow Jesus, step out in faith, but be aware that the enemy plans attacks.

Have you ever experienced unusual crafty enemy attack? Can you see the encouragement that you were being used by God?

36
Shedding dead leaves

Hebrews 12 v 1

"Let us throw off everything that hinders us and the sin that so easily entangles us . . . let us run with perseverance . . ."

When trees discard their leaves in the Autumn they do so to discard the poison from the tree and make the room needed for new growth in Spring.

As the leaves fall, they are carrying away toxic waste. Horses have been known the die inadvertently from eating these dead leaves mixed up with hay. They really do contain concentrated, deadly chemicals.

The text in Hebrews alerts us to let go of anything that we embrace or hold onto, which prevents us from running to our calling in Christ. This includes painful memories that we have a habit of replaying over and over in our minds. It includes co-dependant relationships where both parties accept the poison each put in the other.

The dead leaves are areas of our lives to walk away from. We can get stuck.

Can we identify dead things from the past that we still feed off or guilt we still hang on to?

Let today be the day when we throw off everything, give it to God to handle, and go for growth in the future.

37

Pride steals everything

Obadiah v 3

"The pride of your heart has deceived you, you who live in the clefts of the rocks and make your home on the heights. You who say to yourself, who can bring me down to the ground?"

v 5

"If thieves came to you, if robbers in the night – oh what disaster awaits you – would they not steal only as much as they wanted? . . . But how Esau will be ransacked, his hidden treasures pillaged!"

A few years ago I went out late in the evening. On my return, I found the front door had been locked from the inside. After getting in, I saw that the burglars had left through the backdoor. On further inspection, they had taken a couple of computers. They had also gone through the drawers in my bedroom. The English police came a few days later and checked for finger prints. The burglars had actually used a child to get through a small window to gain entry and unlock the back door to allow easy escape.

Whilst Burglars are generally very selective in what they steal, Obadiah is saying that they will take everything and leave nothing. Not just the "computers" but the furniture, carpets, jewellery, paintings and all else. Pride steals everything. The Edomites were full of pride. They lived in the high places in, what they thought, was impregnable. They were opportunistic. When the Babylonians took Israel into captivity, the Edomites watched and jeered in approval.

But this coming judgement was based on previous incidents. Historically, Israel had tried to pass through the land occupied by the Edomites in order to get to the promised land. When we look back into the book of Numbers (20 v 14) we see how Moses had very respectfully requested to pass through the Edomite territory. Various promises were made to not drink from wells, allow their livestock to graze etc . . . In Deuteronomy, they had also been warned not to go to war with the Edomites. An army came out to defend the Edomite territory and Israel heeded the warning from God and in humility, turned back.

Moses feared God and chose humility. Edom chose pride. Incredibly, there is not one Edomite left on planet earth today, yet Israel flourishes.

Do we regularly humble ourselves before God to ensure that we are protected from the deception of pride?

38
Forgetting who fed me

1 kings 17

"Some time later the son of the woman who owned the house became ill. He grew worse and worse and finally stopped breathing. She said to Elijah "what do you have against me, man of God? Did you come to remind me of my sin and kill my son." "Give me your son," Elijah replied. He took him from her arms . . . "Lord my God let this boy's life return to him."

I am always amazed how easily I forget how good God has been to me in my life. I need to remind myself regularly. The alternative is fear, self-reliance, self protection.

The last time I applied for a job was 30 years ago, but since then I have found the Lord providing work without a struggle. I now find myself with a significant loss of work, yet I still sometimes forget God's faithfulness in the past and don't find peace until I remember and meditate on this.

In the amazing story of 1 kings 17, it is remarkable that the widow of Zarephath was delivered from starvation with a plentiful supply of food that never ran out. Elijah then chooses to lodge in her house.

"Some time later" her son dies and she immediately accuses Elijah with vicious words "what do you have against me, man of God. Did you come to remind me of my sin and kill my son?"

She had forgotten what God had done for her in the past, saving her son and herself from death of starvation with a routinely full stomach. She doesn't realise that the same God who provided food can also provide deliverance from death.

Despite her strong words, Elijah prays and the son lives. She then testifies again to God's goodness.

Interestingly her rescue from starvation came when she gave over what she had to the prophet Elijah. She handed her situation into God's hands. In this passage, she released her son over to Elijah so he could pray for him.

Do we struggle to give our situations over to God and remember and not forget past faithfulness.

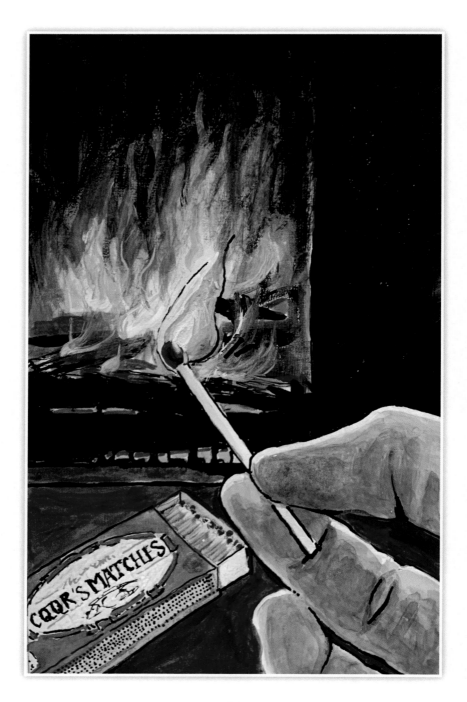

39
Out of the matchbox

2 Timothy 1 v 6

"For this reason I remind you to fan into flame the gift of God which is in you through the laying on of my hands. For God did not give us a spirit of fear but of power, love and a sound mind.

Welcome to a conversation taking place between matches within the darkness of a matchbox: –

Mr Lazy "It's good to be here in the warmth of the matchbox. I heard that our tip bursts into flames when it is struck on the box! It must look good. I'm told that it creates heat. An interesting thought and a nice ability from the master, but I prefer sleep."

Miss indecision "yes I heard that. My friend Suzy offered to be struck, and I saw a glimpse of what happened when she offered herself to the master to be pulled from the box by the big hand!"

Mr Lazy "oh! what happened?"

Miss indecision "Well, I saw her tip burst into flames and set alight a whole log fire – it filled the whole house with warmth and the humans were happy. They like warmth."

Mr Lazy "Sounds good . . . Zzzzzz . . .".

Miss indecision "Sounds really good! I would love to offer myself, but supposing my match doesn't burst into flames. Say it's a faulty match head or maybe something else goes wrong. Perhaps the hand might drop me on the floor. Suppose the floor was damp, my tip would become damp and useless.

Fear is the threat to us using our gifts from God. It was fear that actually kept Miss indecision and Mr Lazy in the box. They never used their gifts within them to set ablaze the fire. Christians should use their gifts to channel the Holy Spirit within them!

Lets accept gods invitation to use our gifts

40
I had a dream

Hebrews 12 v 28-29

"Therefore, since we are receiving a kingdom that cannot be shaken, let us be thankful and so worship God acceptably with reverence and awe. For our God is an all consuming fire"

We are told that when we dream we often don't remember them. I would be one of those people. I often read in the bible that God communicates through dreams and have longed for this. I do however remember just one vivid dream that I believe was from God. I don't recollect any others, so the Lord may have been getting my attention to this one!

In the dream, I saw the street where I lived. Each of the houses had been destroyed with all the roofs ripped off, making them uninhabitable. This had also happened to every car on the street. A strange sight. Then I saw my own house. The car was destroyed, however my house was completely untouched as if whatever had swept by had ignored my property and moved onto the next one!

When I woke up at about 6am, so powerful was the dream and so convinced was I that it had happened, that I went to the window to inspect the damage on the street. Nothing had changed, but I knew God had spoken and began to reflect.

The dream reveals a most humbling truth that is reflected in scripture. The blood of Jesus, which washes away sin. For those who receive Christ, the blood of Jesus protects us. We become his children.

For those who reject Christ they ignore the love of God and the offer of salvation (which is a free gift to those who receive it). In rejecting his love, they are given over to another aspect of God, his all consuming fire which is terrible.

I am writing this blog from Singapore and wrote it after I felt the Lord speak those words "Our God is a consuming fire." I meditated on the scripture the following day and felt greatly empowered and strengthened in my faith. It was as if the compass of my heart was being redirected to see the reality of who God is once more.

I sought to repent of making God into my image rather than his.

When was the last time you asked God to speak to you in a dream?

41
The blessing carriers

John 2 v 8-9

'Then he told them, "now draw some out and take it to the master of the banquet". They did so, and the master of the banquet tasted the water. It had been turned into wine!'

Sometimes, we are called by God to carry out a blessing to others without knowing the impact of what we bring. I recall a time when I had just got on a train to London. I had just heard a great sermon on hearing from God. I remember praying "Jesus I'm willing to do whatever you call me to do." I guess I was surprised when God replied, "go and speak to the man at the end of the carriage". I had heard clearly, but I didn't have the courage to obey.

On arriving in London, I went down the escalator and located the tube line. I sat down on the end bench feeling a failure. Then, to my astonishment, the very person I had seen on the train walked past me and sat down at an empty bench next to mine.

God seemed to nudge me and said "would you like another go?"

I grabbed the opportunity and politely approached the guy.

I said "excuse me, I'm a Christian and I sense I am meant speak to you."
He said "can I ask you a question?"
I said "yes"
He said "do you believe the bible is still true today?"
I said "why do you ask?"
He said "I'm doing something I know the bible says is wrong" . . . "the church leaders have asked me to change."

We call this a divine appointment. We prayed together and I trusted that God had spoken to this man. He looked relieved.

In a sense, like the carriers of the water that was turned into wine, I had to trust that what I was "delivering" was going to taste good. But like the servants, I needed to obey God. When God calls us to step out and obey with clarity, we can be sure he is with us!

Are you willing to take the risk of stepping out in faith to be a blessing carrier?

42
Enforced Listening

Isaiah 41 v 1

"Be silent before me you islands! Let the nations renew their strength!"

There are times in life when God exposes the frailty of the plans of man in order that we refocus our minds on what is important. Most recently the coronavirus has swept through the world causing great issues.

Going back to 2010 I recall the Icelandic volcanic eruption which, although small, left an ash cloud that cancelled nearly 100,000 flights. At the time, I was in Asia on a business trip and found that I could not return to London for three weeks after the planned return date.

The work I had to complete in Asia was finished and therefore I had time to ponder a book I wanted to write because there were no new business objectives. I had felt called by God to write the book, however I never seemed to have the time to start writing it until this enforced period abroad came about. Sometimes events happen in life that God uses to bring about his purpose.

In the text God is calling the nations to listen. God wants us to fulfil the purposes he has in mind for us. Whether it be on an individual basis, or by nation.

Do we seize the time opportunities when God gives them?

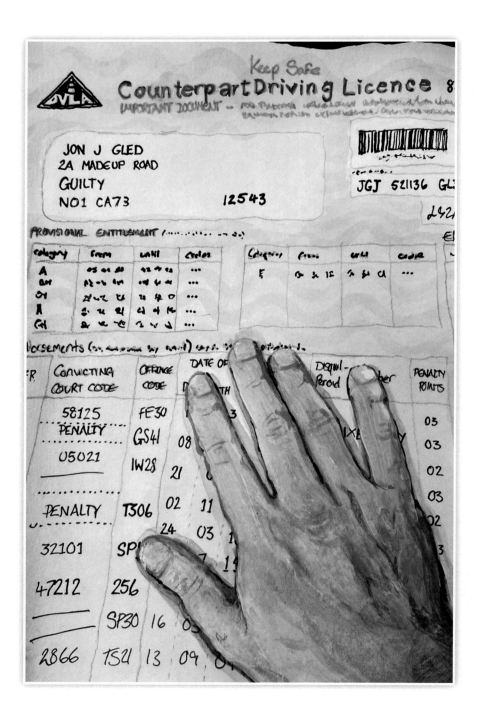

43

Erased Without Trace

1 John 1 v 9

"If we confess our sins, he is faithful and just to forgive our sins, and to cleanse us from all unrighteousness."

Psalm 103 v 12

"As far as the east is from the west, so far has he removed our transgressions from us."

I still have my old paper copy driving licence. It shows all of my old driving mistakes (marked by penalty points) over the last 15 or so years. These were mostly from minor incidents whereby I thought the limit was 40mph but it was actually 30mph.

We are all human and are therefore likely to make mistakes. As the cook said to me when studying at Bible college, "It happens to the best of us."

The mistakes on a driving licence are written off legally after 3 years, but they remain "live" on the licence for a further year. Although we now have card licences, the mistakes are still recorded until they expire after a pre-set time.

How does God see our sins that are technically marks against us? As Christians, our sins past, present and future were removed when we gave our lives to Christ. As far as the east is from the west!

We serve a God who does not hold grudges. Who does not call us to account for previous sins because of Jesus' defeat of sin on the cross!

So, given that our "penalty points" are removed, why do we struggle so often to forgive the faults of others when they wrong us?

Or do we also struggle forgiving ourselves?

44
Fully Insured

Matthew 16 v 24-25

"Then Jesus said to his disciples, 'Whoever wants to be my disciple must deny themselves and take up their cross and follow me. For . . . whoever loses their life for me will find it.'"

John 6 v 66

"From that time onwards, many disciples followed him no more."

I used to drive a company car as part of my job and frequently used motorways. One day, whilst driving between cities, I noticed a sudden change in the car's performance and, soon after, I could smell smoke.

I pulled over onto the hard-shoulder and got out of the car – the smoke became stronger and I walked hurriedly away! I stood away from the stream of cars racing by, staring at my smoking car. Suddenly it was ablaze. I was stunned to see this modern high-performance car melt before my eyes, but more so, grateful to God that I was able to escape the car's blaze and certain death.

Following this incident, the insurance teams clarified that the cause was a catastrophic failure of the fly wheel, a critical component of the engine. The insurance was therefore paid out against a claim.

Life is frail.

We need to put our confidence in someone who never changes.

In the texts given, Jesus is describing the Christian life of sacrifice and service. His insurance policy is different.

Whoever loses his life – will find it. That, perhaps, is why some disciples took a look at what was on offer and decided that the walk Jesus was describing in his teaching insured them for something they didn't really want (see John 6 v 66).

We have no guarantee for today, neither tomorrow or our safety in the world. We need to put our trust in Christ who insures us from the impact of sin by giving eternal life.

Let's check that we are still following the insurance policy of Jesus.

45
The God Connections

John 10 v 27

"My sheep listen to my voice; I know them, and they follow me."

There are times in our lives when we don't look to God for help. Often the help God wants to give, opens up an opportunity for the Lord to share his heart with those who need to hear from him. So often, I don't tune into his voice and see him opening up life to others.

I recall a time when I was working on my business and became aware of a need for a French speaker to help with translation or making phone calls. I was pondering this as I walked down to the train station one day and had a sense of God speaking.

"Ask the man who serves the coffee."

There was a small shop serving coffee for passengers preparing to board trains. I recalled that the previous people I had seen there were likely to be from French-speaking North Africa.

The conversation in the shop followed:

"Hello, do you know anyone who speaks French and would like to do translation work?"

"Well I do, but unfortunately I'm too busy. I do, however, know a friend who could help you."

He took my number and I received a call from his friend a day later.

We proceeded to meet in town and chat about the opportunity. We became friends and he engaged with people I knew at my church. One day, to my surprise, he called me to ask if we could meet in town. He shared:

"Jon, last night I had a dream. A very tall man approached me in the dream, shining white and with arms wide open. He called my name and said, 'My name is Jesus. Nice to meet you. I forgive you.'"

My friend woke from the dream with a strong sense of peace.

From then on, my friend encountered Jesus in many ways and went on to do an Alpha course. I realised that obeying God's voice was key to seeing the miracles of God emerge. God wants to supply our everyday needs and extend the gospel at the same time.

46
Order from Chaos

Genesis 1 v 2-3

"Now the earth was formless and empty, darkness was over the surface of the deep, and the Spirit of God was hovering over the waters. And God said, 'Let there be light.'"

I recall lending my home to a group of film writers who needed to find a context where they could complete the first part of their work. I knew them, and happily went out for the day to allow them to complete their work.

When I got home I saw what looked like a group of students had invaded. The lounge was in the kitchen, the bedroom in the utility room, the kitchen on the stairs . . . Initially the shock was bad, but after the filming was over, order was restored.

In Genesis, we see the account of the creation of the world. What was formless and void, is transformed to order from chaos.

When we see the mental health crisis in the world, we see a breakdown of well-being in people unable to connect their lives together. Their minds are disconnected and so they need the light of Jesus.

Jesus brings chaos into order. This is made possible through the indwelling work of the Holy Spirit.

Sometimes we feel that life is chaotic and out of order and don't know which way to turn. When things look like they are void and formless, the good news is that we can access the God of order simply by calling on him.

47
Root and Fruit Growth

Jeremiah 17 v 7-8

"Blessed is the one who trusts in the Lord, whose confidence is in him. They will be like a tree planted by the water that sends out its roots by the stream. It does not fear when the heat comes ... It has no worries in a year of drought and never fails to bear fruit."

I used to grow tomato plants as a kid. The plants needed to be grown in small pots with added water and nutrients, protected from the outside world. This care was essential when kept in sunny areas indoors.

However, there comes a time when the plant needs to leave the comfort and security of the pot to grow large and strong out in the wild. The issue is the fruit-bearing that God invites us to embrace. Good fruit is a by-product of root quality.

There is a nurturing phase to the Christian life too, where the level of protection needs to be at a higher standard, in a pot. Vital nutrients, such as learning about the gospel and God's unconditional love, are added to ensure that the initial growth is of a high quality.

For the Christian, when God calls us to grow and takes us out of the small pot, there is a risk element, and the challenges are multi-faceted. We will initially experience discomfort as the roots grow much deeper, this being necessary to teach us to trust, to lean on him in adversity and to thus hold the increasing fruit of this faith going forth.

As Christians, we can resist God's invitation to grow and a sad issue today is that older Christians are still living in the confines of their small pots and never accept the invitation to grow. This means that they will never be able to fulfil the full extent of growth that God has planned for them. However, the good news is that God allows painful discipline to come upon our lives in order to force the growth phase. This can be very hard.

When the hand of God reaches down to our small pot and invites us to move to the bigger thing, will we accept his invitation?

Let's ponder whether God is inviting us to grow in our faith and accept the call to move to the bigger pot. Is it a business that we have resisted starting? Asking real questions to strengthen a marriage? Stepping into a gifting that you have been too shy to use? Ask the Lord today and grow your roots!

48
Stepping into God's Provision

Mark 11 v 24

"Therefore I tell you, whatever you ask for in prayer, believe that you have received it, and it will be yours."

My biggest strength is my biggest vulnerability. When I find myself needing something, I am fairly resourceful in "making it happen". This of course is fine, but God wants us to know that he is the ultimate provider for his children. The Lord desires us to know that we can ask him for anything, and trust in his ability to provide.

Some years ago, I was overseas, having recently lost my job. I was with a friend, Roland, who drove me out towards an area to shop. One of the reasons for going was to get a new mobile as I had needed to return my old company phone.

As we drove, we saw that the car park was almost empty and therefore chose a random parking spot. I muttered a prayer out loud which was hardly faith filled, "Lord I need a phone . . . (sigh)."

Now what happened next was something that had never happened to me before. Before you read what follows, take a deep breath . . .

When I opened the passenger door, I saw that I had stepped into a pile of national currency notes which were spread out on the floor. I was stunned and announced the miracle to Roland. He opened his door and stepped into a spread of notes on his side too. He said, "Ah . . . thank you, Jesus," as if it was normal. I was amazed as I hadn't experienced a miracle like that before, ever, and am usually somewhat sceptical. We scooped up the money and bought the phone with a joyful sense that God had answered my muttered prayer.

The notes stood out against the ground, therefore we would have seen so many before parking, but hadn't seen a thing. As I pondered this, I sensed the Lord sharing with me that an angel had been sent at "angel high speed", and placed the currency on the ground. The notes were arranged so perfectly at the speed of light.

So why is this significant? Twofold.

The quality of my prayer for a phone was really a sigh . . . a tired child of God. No formula. No articulate prayer. God was showing me that heaven hears the weakest prayer and that Jesus can answer prayer immediately.

Secondly, it shows me that God is watching his children and he wants to show us sometimes that we don't have to make it happen in our own strength.

So, for all of us, we need to expect our Lord to provide for us in many ways when he knows we are in need.

Do you and I live in that expectancy? You never know what you might find.

49
Sun Protection

Mark 4 v 32

"Yet when planted, it [mustard seed] grows and becomes the largest of all the garden plants, with such big branches that the birds can perch in its shade."

Many years ago, I bought a bird table for my mother's birthday. I was pleased with its height and the little roof fitted to the top perfectly too. In the winter, when snow covered the ground, the birds flocked to the table to eat the nuts that she placed there. The nuts provided relief from the search for food when all that could be seen was snow and ice. In the summer, the birds just flew by the table as food was visible and plentiful. Summer life is easy for birds – winter can be very challenging.

The parable reflects the growth of the kingdom of God. Starting small but finishing big. In fact, mustard seeds can grow into trees of up to 30 feet tall.

The birds fly into the branches, not for food, but to enjoy the shade of the leaves and freedom from the oppressive heat in the Middle East.

The birds in many ways represent the vulnerable, the needy, the unemployed, the sick, the lonely, those going through divorce and so on. As believers in Christ, we have the capacity to serve those in need and protect them from the oppressive heat of the demands of life. We are the leaves.

We see that our influence as believers grows with the kingdom as we provide leaves of protection within the many spheres of life. Leaves of protection are multi-facetted. We all need to ask God to show us what our bird tables look like. How can we serve others and bring God's kingdom?

Can we build bigger bird tables and expand our capacity to protect?

Can we see how we can be those branches of protection?

50
Surprised by the Spirit of God

Zephaniah 3 v 17

"The Lord your God is in your midst, the mighty warrior who saves."

A few years ago, I was returning to the UK from Singapore via the Middle East, where I stopped over for a few days to meet our company agent. In the morning, I awoke with an unusual awareness of the presence of God filling the hotel room. This was unusual in the sense of its strength. I just prayed, "Lord, whatever you are up to today I make myself available to you."

I got ready to leave the hotel and was picked up by my local agent. We went to a well-known coffee shop downtown and discussed a few projects. My agent then said, "Jon, I want to share something with you but we need to discuss this back in the car." On returning to the car, he proceeded to play the car audio. He had downloaded the whole of the New Testament. Knowing that I was a Christian, he then asked me, "Jon, why did you become a Christian? What's it like? I need to ask you here in the car as I cannot attend a church."

The Holy Spirit moves on his people to get their attention and empower them for purpose. We live in a culture increasingly oriented towards feelings and emotions for the sake of feelings and emotions. One of the alarming trends in the church has been the experience of the presence of God with no tangible purpose. This is simply not the case in the Bible. For example, in Acts we hear that the disciples were called to wait in Jerusalem where they would receive power from above to do the works of God.

As I thought about this exciting encounter with God and the clear opening provided to testify, I pondered whether I am walking in the expectation of seeing God move in power.

How about yourself?

Have you seen or experienced the Holy Spirit preparing you to serve the Kingdom?

As Zephaniah says, God is near and mighty to save!

51

When it Doesn't Taste Good

Revelation 3 v 15-16

"I know your deeds, that you are neither cold nor hot. I wish that you were either one or the other! So, because you are lukewarm – neither hot nor cold – I am about to spit you out of my mouth."

How often have I made a mug of hot tea, taken a first sip, then a phone call comes and I am in conversation for a good half an hour. On returning to my drink, I find it to be lukewarm and very undesirable. However, hot tea or iced tea has a distinct flavour of its own. Both are good. Try mixing the two teas and the result is awful.

In the first three chapters of Revelation, we have seven letters from Jesus to seven churches, currently part of Turkey.

Having lived in Turkey, I have seen the cold and the heat. I used to hear sermons encouraging people to be "hot for God" in contrast to a "cold heart" that is far from God. The preacher would urge people to be passionately in love with the Lord and hot rather than backslidden and cold.

However, this is not actually a correct interpretation of the text. Laodicea did not have a good water source. It received hot water from the north from the city of Hierapolis, famous for its healing hot springs. In contrast, refreshing cold water came from the south in Colossae, sourced from the mountains where snow melted to give a refreshing drink in the heat of day.

The key thing that Jesus points to is that the two streams of water had lost their distinctive benefits. No longer hot and healing, or cold and refreshing. The long journey to Laodicea meant that the great benefits of the healing hot water or refreshing chilled streams had been neutralised en route, rendering them useless.

How relevant is this to a modern westernised nation?

Laodicea had a great reputation with a top medical school and clothing industry. It was self-sufficient not God sufficient.

We need to be real. We can go to our church buildings, live a life with an appearance of zeal but be far from God.

Let's get before God and seek his heart. Let's ask him to shine his light in our hearts and then apply change. Let's be God sufficient.

52

When We Trip Over Ourselves

Psalm 19 v 14

"May these words of my mouth and this meditation of my heart be pleasing in your sight, Lord, my Rock and my Redeemer."

I used to make business trips across the Middle East and I recall one trip in particular when sat next to a fairly vocal passenger. I had pulled out a book I was reading on the importance of prayer, and quietly sat there with the coffee provided. The gentleman next to me struck up a conversation and asked me what I was reading. The conversation commenced:

Passenger: "What are you reading about?"
Me: "Prayer."
Passenger: "So you are a Christian?"
Me: "I am."

Then he explained to me that he was also a Christian and proceeded to contrast English churches with those in his country.

Passenger: "So how many people go to your prayer meetings in England?"
Me: "Thirty or so."
Passenger: "Thirty! We have a thousand! **Do you really know the Lord? Do you really trust God?**" – Was he thinking that I might not be a Christian?
Me: "Well that's great to hear! Yes, we are not really in revival these days."
Passenger: "How many people go to your Sunday services?"
Me: "About a hundred and fifty or so."
Passenger: "A hundred and fifty! We have ten thousand!" "**Do you really trust God . . .?**"

As we descended to land, we swapped numbers to keep in contact because I was amazed about what I had heard! A few days later, further to checking in to my hotel, I received a text from him. To my astonishment it read, "How are you, dear brother? I need to ask you to receive the Lord's blessing by paying my hotel bill"! – did He trust God?

I was stunned and pondered how this text could be so different to what I had experienced of his personality on the plane.

The Bible verse above calls all Christians to be self-aware and live a whole life of unity in terms of what we say and our heart condition.

This is a challenge for me as I am very aware of the danger of being unaware of this. I can trip over myself.

How are you doing?